CHRISTMAS RECIPES

ISBN-13: 978-1494421939

ISBN-10: 1494421933

INTRODUCTION

Christmas food is something unique and different from other times of the year, because of the many efforts that go into making varieties of rich dishes for our family and friends and for Christmas parties. You can find many recipes for your Christmas entertaining needs; from Appetizers, Baking, Main Meals, Desserts and side dishes.

APPETIZERS AND SNACKS

11 ounce Fresh Goat Cheese Log

1 sheet frozen puff pastry dough

1 egg, beaten (for egg wash)

1 cup dried cranberries or cherries

1 fresh rosemary sprig, roughly chopped

Directions

Thaw puff pastry according to package directions. Spread 1 sheet puff pastry on flat work surface; arrange dried cranberries or cherries in center in a 6 inch square shape. Sprinkle chopped rosemary over cherries. Place Goat Cheese Log in the center of prepared puff pastry round side down.

Brush egg wash onto uncovered sides of pastry. Begin wrapping sides of pastry around the Goat Cheese Log gently pressing at the overlap to seal well. Pinch ends of pastry firmly around the cheese and trim excess pastry.

Place on a sheet tray and refrigerate a minimum of 1 hour. Preheat oven to 375 degrees F. Bake 10-15 minutes, until golden brown.

Cool 10 minutes before serving.

PINE CONE CHEESE BALLS

2 cups shredded Swiss cheese

½ cup butter

3 Tablespoons milk

2 Tablespoons dry sherry or milk

1/8 teaspoon ground red pepper

1 cup finely chopped blanched almonds

¾ cup sliced almonds

½ cup whole almonds

Rosemary

Crackers

Directions

1. Beat cheese, butter, milk, sherry, and red pepper in a medium bowl until smooth; stir in chopped almonds.

2. Divide mixture into 3 equal portions; shape each into tapered ovals to resemble pine cones. Insert slivered, sliced and whole almonds into the cones. Cover and refrigerate 2 to 3 hours or until firm.

3. Arrange pine cones on wooden cheese board or serving platter. Garnish with rosemary. Serve with crackers

Makes 12 to 16 appetizer servings

1 (8-oz) pkg. cream cheese, softened

1 (8-oz) pkg. sharp Cheddar cheese

¾ cup crumbled blue cheese

¼ cup chopped green onions

2 Tablespoons milk

1 teaspoon Worcestershire sauce

Finely chopped walnuts or pecans

Directions

1. Mix cheeses, green onions, milk and Worcestershire sauce until well blended. Refrigerate 1 to 2 hours.

2. Shape into a ball; roll in chopped walnuts. Serve with apple slices or crackers.

Makes 2-2/3 cups

CHRISTMAS APPETIZER PUFFS

1 sheet frozen puff pastry, thawed (half 17 ½ -oz. package)

2 Tablespoons olive oil or vegetable oil

Toppings: Parmesan cheese, sesame seeds, poppy seeds, dried dill weed, dried basil leaves, paprika, stuffed green olive slices

Directions

1. Preheat oven to 425 degrees F. Roll pastry on lightly floured surface to 13-inch square. Cut into shapes with cookie cutters (simple-shaped cutters work best, like Christmas trees bells and stars etc. Place on ungreased baking sheet.

2. Brush cut-outs lightly with oil. Decorate with desired toppings.

3. Bake 6 to 8 minutes or until golden, serve warm or room temperature,

Makes 18 appetizers

1 dozen large eggs, hard-cooked and peeled

6 Tablespoons mayonnaise

3 Tablespoons pickled sliced jalapeño peppers, minced

1 Tablespoon mustard

1/2 teaspoon cumin

1/8 teaspoon salt

Garnish: chopped fresh cilantro

Directions

Cut eggs in half lengthwise and carefully remove yolks. Mash yolks; stir in mayonnaise and next 4 ingredients. Spoon or pipe; egg yolk mixture into egg white halves. Cover and chill at least 1 hour or until ready to serve. Garnish, if desired.

Makes 24 deviled eggs

Note: Fresh eggs are harder to peel: Buy eggs and refrigerate 7 to 10 days for easy peeling.

CHEESY CHRISTMAS TREES

½ cup mayonnaise

1 Tablespoon dry ranch-style salad dressing

1 cup shredded cheddar cheese

¼ cup grated parmesan cheese

12 slices firm white bread

¼ cup red pepper strips

¼ cup green bell pepper strips

Directions

1. Preheat broiler: Combine mayonnaise and salad dressing mix in a medium bowl. Add cheeses; mix well.

2. Cut bread slices into Christmas tree shapes using large cookie cutter. Spread each tree with about 1 Tablespoon mayo mixture. Decorate with red and green bell pepper strips. Place on baking sheet.

3. Broil 4 inches from heat 2 to 3 minutes or until bubbling. Serve warm.

Makes 12 appetizers

2 cups oatmeal cereal squares

12 cups corn cereal squares

2 cups mini pretzels

1 cup whole almonds

¼ cup butter

1/3 cup frozen orange juice concentrate, thawed

3 Tablespoon packed brown sugar

1 teaspoon ground cinnamon

¾ teaspoon ground ginger

¼ teaspoon ground nutmeg

2/3 cup dried cranberries

Directions

1. Preheat oven to 250 degrees F. Spray 13 x 9-inch baking pan with nonstick cooking spray.

2. Combine cereal squares, pretzels and almonds in a large bowl, set aside.

3. Melt butter in medium microwave bowl on HIGH 45 to 60 seconds, Stir in orange juice concentrate, brown sugar, cinnamon, ginger and nutmeg until well blended, Pour over cereal mixture; stir well to coat. Place in prepared pan and spread to one layer.

4. Bake 50 minutes, stirring every 10 minutes. Stir in cranberries. Let cool in pan on wire rack, leaving uncovered until mixture is crisp. Store in airtight container or plastic storage bag

Makes 8 Cups

SANTA FE TRAIL MIX

1 ½ cups pecans halves

1 cup cashews

¾ cup roasted shelled pistachio nuts

½ cup pine nuts

1/3 cup roasted sunflower seeds

3 Tablespoons butter

2 ½ teaspoons ground cumin

¼ teaspoon garlic powder

¼ cup plus 1 Tbsp. chili sauce

1 chipotle Chile in adobo sauce, about 3-inch long

1 Tablespoon frozen orange juice concentrate, thawed

Cooking spray

1 Tablespoon dried cilantro, divided

Directions

1. Preheat oven to 300 degrees F. Line 14 x11-inch baking sheet with foil, set aside

2. Combine pecans, cashews, pistachios, pine nuts and sunflower seeds in a large bowl.

3. Combine butter, cumin and garlic powder in small microwavable bowl. Microwave on High 45 to 50 seconds or until butter is melted and foamy; stir to blend.

4. Place butter mixture, chili sauce, chipotle Chile and orange juice concentrate in food processor or blender; process until smooth. Pour sauce over nut mixture; stir to evenly coat. Spread mixture in single layer on prepared baking sheet.

5. Bake about 1 hour, stirring every 10 minutes. Remove from oven and spray mixture evenly with cooking spray. Sprinkle 1 ½ teaspoons cilantro over mixture. Stir mixture with spatula and repeat with additional cooking spray and remaining cilantro. Set baking sheet on wire rack to cool. Leave uncovered at least 1 hour before storing in airtight container or resealable plastic bag.

KALE CHIPS

1 bunch of kale, washed and stems removed

2 Tablespoons apple cider vinegar or lime juice

2 Tablespoon olive oil

Sea salt or Himalayan salt

Directions

1. Preheat oven to 350 degrees F

.

2. Chop or tear kale into pieces. In a bowl combine vinegar, oil and salt; mix well with kale and massage into kale pieces.

3. Spread onto baking sheet. Bake for 10 minutes or until crispy. Take kale out immediately if it changes color to brown.

2 cups (8-oz) shredded cheddar cheese

½ cup grated parmesan cheese

½ cup sunflower oil margarine, softened

3 Tablespoons water

1 cup all-purpose flour

¼ teaspoon salt, optional

1 cup uncooked quick oats

2/3 cup roasted, salted sunflower seeds

Directions

In a bowl beat cheeses, margarine and water until blended. Mix in flour and salt. Stir in oats and sunflower seeds until combined. Shape into a 12-inch-long roll; wrap securely. Refrigerate about 4 hours or up to 1 week.

Preheat oven to 400 degrees F. Lightly grease cookie sheets. Cut roll into 1/8 to ¼-inch slices; flatten each slice slightly. Place on prepared cookie sheets. Bake 8 to 10 minutes or until edges are light golden brown. Remove immediately; cool on wire racks.

Makes about 4 to 5 dozen

CHEESE TWISTS

1 cup all-purpose flour

½ teaspoon baking powder

½ teaspoon dry ground mustard

½ teaspoon salt

1/8 teaspoon ground red pepper

¾ cup grated parmesan cheese, divided

½ cup butter or margarine, softened

3 egg yolks

2 teaspoons water

1 egg white lightly beaten

1 Tablespoon sesame seeds, optional

Directions

Preheat oven to 400 degrees F, Grease 2 cookie sheets

In a large bowl, combine flour, baking powder, mustard, salt and red pepper. Reserve 1 Tablespoons cheese; stir remaining cheese into flour mixture. Cut in butter with pastry blender or 2 knives or even your fingertips until mixture resembles fine crumbs. Add egg yolks and water, mixing until dough forms. Shape into a ball; flatten and wrap in plastic wrap. Refrigerate 2 hours or until firm.

Roll out dough on lightly floured surface into a 12-inch square (about 1/8-inch thick) Brush surface lightly with egg white and sprinkle with remaining 1 Tablespoon parmesan cheese and sesame seeds, if desired. Cut dough in half. Cut each half crosswise into ¼-inch stripes. Twist 2 strips together. Repeat with remaining strips. Place 1-inch apart on prepared cookie sheets.

Bake 6 to 8 minutes or until lightly golden brown. Remove from cookie sheets and cool completely on wire racks. Store in air tight container

Makes about 48 twists

CHEDDAR-PECAN CRIPS

16 ounces medium sharp cheese, shredded

¼ cup butter or margarine

2 cups all-purpose flour

2 cups Rice Krispies cereal

Pecan halves

Red pepper to taste

Seasoning Salt to taste

Directions

1. Preheat oven to 350 degrees F.

2. Allow cheese and butter to reach room temperature. In a large bowl cream together; add red pepper to taste. Add flour and mix. Stir in Rice Krispies with a wooden spoon and mix to combine.

3. Take small pieces of dough and make into a ball similar to making cookies. If dough is hard to handle; chill in the refrigerator before handling.

4. Place ball on cookie sheet and flatten with a fork. Top with a pecan half and sprinkle with seasoned salt.

5. Bake for about 10 minutes. Cool and store in air tight container.

Makes about 48

1 (10-oz) can refrigerated pizza crust

1 cup (4-oz) shredded mozzarella cheese

½ (3.5-oz) pkg. sliced pepperoni, chopped

½ cup spaghetti sauce

Directions

1. Unroll refrigerated pizza crust on a cutting board; sprinkle with cheese and pepperoni. Roll up, starting with long side; moisten edges with water, and pinch edges to seal.

2. Place in freezer for 20 minutes to make cutting easier. Cut into 2-inch slices and place 1 inch apart in a lightly greased 15x10x1-inch jellyroll pan; flatten slightly.

3. Bake at 400 degrees F: for 15 to 20 minutes; serve with warm spaghetti sauce, if desired. My 5 year-old grandson like's ranch dressing

Makes 8 Servings

Note: Baked Pinwheels can be stored in an airtight container in the refrigerator for up to 1 week, or may be frozen and slices and baked when you are ready. As in step 2

CINNAMON TWISTS

4 1/3 cups all-purpose flour

1 pkg. Active dry yeast

1 cup milk

1/3 cup Butter or Margarine

1/3 cup Sugar

2 ½ teaspoons cinnamon

½ teaspoon salt

2 eggs

Glaze:

1 cup powdered sugar

¼ teaspoon milk

1 Tablespoon milk

Directions

1. Combine 2 cups flour with yeast.

2. Heat and stir milk, butter or margarine, sugar and salt until warm and butter is almost melted.

3. Add this to the flour mixture, add the eggs.

4. Beat with an electric mixer on low speed for 30 seconds, scraping the bowl, then beat on high speed for approx. 3 minutes. Stir in as much of the remaining flour (2 to 2 1/3 cups) as you can; scraping sides.

5. Turn out onto a lightly floured surface. Knead in enough remaining flour to make a smooth and elastic (about 3 - 5 minutes). Shape into a ball. Place in a lightly greased bowl. Cover and let rise in a warm place till double in size. (About 1 hour)

6. Punch dough down. Divide in half. Cover and let rest 10 minutes.

7. Roll each half of the dough into a 12 x 8 inch rectangle. Melt 3 tablespoons butter or margarine; brush half over the dough. Combine ¾ cup sugar and 2 ½ teaspoons ground cinnamon; sprinkle half of the mixture over dough. Fold dough in half and then in half again, repeat with second dough. Cut strips of dough along the short end and twist sealing the seams.

8. Preheat oven to 375 degrees F. Place in a baking sheet. Cover; let rise till nearly double about 30 minutes.

9. Bake in preheated oven. oven for 20 to 25 minutes. (Be sure to check them, they brown easily.)

For the sugar glaze: Combine 1 cup sifted powdered sugar with ¼ teaspoon vanilla and 1 Tablespoon milk. Continue to add milk 1 teaspoon at a time until you get a drizzling consistency.

Makes 8 Servings

BLUEBERRY-LEMON-CREAM LOAF

This recipe is our favorite recipe; great for any occasion

1 (8-oz) pkg. cream cheese, softened

½ cup butter or margarine, softened

1 ¼ cup sugar

2 eggs

2 ¼ cups all-purpose flour

1 Tablespoon baking powder

½ teaspoon salt

¾ cup milk or buttermilk

1 cup fresh or frozen blue berries

1 Tablespoon grated lemon peel

Glaze

1 teaspoon grated lemon rind

2 to 3 Tablespoons lemon juice

1/3 cup sifted powdered sugar

Directions

1. Preheat oven to 350 degrees F. Grease and lightly floured two 8 ½ x 4 ½ x3 loaf pans.

2. Combine cream cheese and butter, blend well. Gradually add sugar; beating until light and fluffy. Add eggs, one at a time, beating mixture well after each addition.

3. Combine flour, baking powder and salt; add to creamed mixture alternately with milk, beginning and ending with flour mixture. Mix well after each addition. Stir in blueberries and lemon peel

4. Pour batter in prepared pans. Bake for 45 minutes or until toothpick inserted comes out clean.

Glaze: Combine lemon peel, lemon juice and powdered sugar, mixing until smooth; pour over hot loaves. Cool in pans for 10to 15 minutes; transfer to wire racks to cool completely.

Makes 2 loaves

CRANBERRY NUT BREAD

This festive, fruity quick bread has become a favorite Thanksgiving and Christmas gift. The cranberries give the bread a juicy, tart bite that offsets the sweet, cakey crumb. This recipe can be easily adapted to make muffins as well as many other flavored loaves

1 Tablespoon oil, to grease pan

1¾ unbleached flour plus extra to dust pan

1½ teaspoons baking powder

½ teaspoons baking soda

½ teaspoon salt

½ cup (60g) pecans, coarsely chopped

1 egg, beaten

¼ cup milk

2/3 cup sugar

4 Tablespoons unsalted butter, melted

1½ cups (175g) cranberries

Directions

1. Grease a 9in x 5in x 3in (22x12x7cm) loaf pan with oil. Dust generously with flour.

Preheat oven to 350 degrees F. (180 C)

2. Sift the flour, baking powder, baking soda, and salt in a large bowl. Stir in the pecans and make a well in the center. Place the remaining ingredients in a separate bowl and mix until thoroughly combined.

3. Pour the mixture and the cranberries into the well. Use a spatula to gently fold all ingredients together to form a wet batter (Over-mixing can result in a heavy batter)

4. Spoon the batter into the prepared loaf pan. Bake in the preheated oven for 1 hour, until golden and well-risen. The bread is ready when the edges shrink from the sides of the pan, and tooth pick inserted into the center comes out clean.

5. Keep the bread in the pan and let stand, about 10 minutes. Carefully run a knife around the edges and turn out. Cool on wire rack.

MACADAMIA NUT BREAD

Traditional banana bread gets tropical flair from macadamia nuts. This quick bread is easy to make. Feel free to substitute your favorite nuts for the macadamias.

2 ¼ cups all-purpose flour

¼ cup granulated sugar

¾ cup brown sugar, firmly packed

3 ½ teaspoons baking powder

½ teaspoon salt

1½ teaspoons ground cinnamon

1¼ cups mashed ripe bananas

1/3 cup milk

1 teaspoon vinegar

3 Tablespoons vegetable oil

1 egg

1 cup macadamia nuts, chopped

Directions

1. Preheat oven to 350 degrees F. Generously grease a 9 x 5-inch loaf pan; set aside.

2. In a large bowl, combine flour, sugar, brown sugar, baking powder, salt, cinnamon, bananas, milk, vinegar, vegetable oil, and egg. Beat at medium speed of electric mixer for 30 seconds or until dry ingredients are just moistened. Stir in macadamia nuts. Spoon batter into prepared loaf pan

3. Bake at 350 degrees F. for 60 to 70 minutes or until wooden pick inserted in center comes out clean. Cool in pan on wire rack for 10 minutes, then remove from pan and cool completely on wire rack before slicing.

QUINOA ZUCCHINI BREAD

2/3 cup coconut oil, melted

3 eggs

1 ½ cups sugar

2 cups zucchini, grated

1 teaspoon baking powder

½ teaspoon baking soda

1 teaspoon salt

1 teaspoon vanilla extract

1 Tablespoon cinnamon

1 cup quinoa flour

1 cup white whole wheat flour

Directions

Preheat oven to 350 degrees. Grease and flour two 9 x 5 loaf pans

Using an electric mixer bowl, beat together the coconut oil, eggs, and sugar. Add the remaining ingredients and beat just until blended. Spoon half of the mixture into each prepared loaf pan.

Sprinkle each loaf with sugar (this step is optional), Bake for 45-50 minutes, or until the center of each loaf springs back when touched lightly with the tip of your finger.

Cool before serving; serve with butter & strawberry jam or whipped cream cheese, if desired Makes 2 loaves

6 large eggs

1/3 cup heavy cream (or coconut milk for Paleo)

¼ cup plus 2 Tablespoons organic whole cane sugar (or ¼ cup honey for Paleo/Primal)

1 teaspoon vanilla extract

1 stick unsalted butter, melted

¾ cup coconut flour

2 teaspoons baking powder

1 teaspoon baking soda

¾ teaspoon sea salt

1 cup cooked and pureed pumpkin

5 ounces mini chocolate chips

Directions:

Preheat oven to 400 degrees F. Adjust rack to middle position. Line muffin pan with muffin liners.

Whisk eggs, cream (or coconut milk), vanilla and butter in a large mixing bowl. In another bowl sift coconut flour, baking powder, baking soda, and salt. Add dry ingredients to wet and whisk until no lumps remain. Fold in pumpkin and chocolate. Spoon batter into muffin cups. Bake for 15 minutes, until golden brown on top. Cool. Store muffins in an airtight container for 3 days Makes 24 Muffins

CHRISTMAS PRETZEL DANISH

½ cup warm milk

1 Tablespoon sugar

1 (.25 ounce) envelope active dry yeast

1 cup heavy cream

3 ½ cups all-purpose flour

1/4 cup sugar

1 teaspoon salt

1 teaspoon ground cardamom

½ cup butter

1 (8 ounce) can almond paste

½ cup crushed sliced almonds

½ cup sugar

1 teaspoon ground cinnamon

1 teaspoon almond extract

½ cup white sugar

1 egg white, beaten

½ cup sliced almonds

Directions

1. In a small bowl, blend together the milk and sugar. Sprinkle the yeast over the top and let stand for 10 minutes to dissolve. Stir in cream.

2. In a separate bowl, mix together the flour, sugar, salt and cardamom. Cut in the butter using a pastry blender or pinching with your fingers until it is a course bread crumb texture. Stir in the yeast mixture until well blended. Pat into a ball, flatten slightly, and then wrap in plastic wrap. Refrigerate for 12 to 24 hours.

3. To make the filling, with an electric mixer, blend the almond paste, almonds, sugar, cinnamon and almond extract until evenly blended. It may be crumbly.

4. Roll the chilled dough out into a 2 inch wide and 24 inch long rectangle. Spread the filling to within 2 inches of the sides and roll up into a tube. Cover surface with sugar, and roll the tube of dough in the sugar to coat thoroughly. Roll and stretch the dough out to form a long rope about 40 inches long. Place on a parchment lined baking sheet and shape into a pretzel shape.

5. Brush the top of the pretzel with egg white and sprinkle with almonds. Cover loosely with a towel and let rise for 45 minutes.

6. Meanwhile: Preheat the oven to 375 degrees F. Bake the pretzel in the preheated oven until golden brown, 25 to 30 minutes. Cut into slices to serve.

PANDORO

This classic Italian bread is traditionally baked in a tall, star- pan. If you can't find one, use an 8-inch springform pan instead. "Sponge" takes on a new meaning in this recipe; it's a yeast mixture used like a starter for this bread

'Sponge" recipe below

1 teaspoon active dry yeast

1 Tablespoon warm water (105 to 115 degrees F)

6 ½ cups bread flour, divided

¼ cup sugar

2 large eggs

¼ cup butter, softened and cut into pieces

4 large eggs

2 egg yolks

1 cup sugar

1 teaspoon salt

2 teaspoon vanilla extract

1 ½ Tablespoons grated lemon rind

1 ¼ cups butter or margarine, softened and cut into pieces

½ cup chopped candied citron

¼ to ½ cups bread flour

Butter-flavored cooking spray

Directions

1. Prepare "sponge" according to recipe, and set aside.

2. Combine yeast and warm water in a 1-cup liquid measuring cup; let stand 5 minutes. Stir yeast mixture, 2½ cups flour, ¼ cup sugar, and 2 eggs into "sponge"; stir vigorously with a wooden spoon until blended. Gradually stir in ¼ cup butter. Cover and let rise in a warm place (85 degrees f.). Free from drafts. 45 minutes or until dough has doubled in size:

3. Add 4 eggs and next 5 ingredients; beat at medium speed with electric mixer until smooth. Gradually add 2 cups flour, beating until blended. Stir in remaining 2 cups of flour with a wooden spoon. Gradually stir in 1 ¼ cups butter and citron.

4. Turn dough out onto a heavily floured surface, and knead until smooth and elastic (about 5 minutes), adding an additional ¼ to ½ cup bread flour, if needed. Place in a well-greased bowl, turning to grease top. Cover and let rise in a warm place 1 ½ hours or until doubled in size.

5. Punch dough down, and divide in half; place in two pandoro pans or 8-inch springform pans coated with cooking spray. Cover and let rise in a warm place (85 degrees F.) Free from drafts, for 1½ hours or until doubled in size. Bake at 350 degrees F. for 30 minutes. Cover with foil, and reduce heat to 300 degrees F.; bake an additional 20 minutes. Makes 2 loaves

"Sponge"

2 packages active dry yeast

½ cup warm water (105 to 115 degrees F)

1 large egg

2 Tablespoons sugar

¾ cup bread flour

Directions

Combine yeast and warm water in a 1-cup measuring cup; let stand 5 minutes. Combine yeast mixture and remaining ingredients in a large mixing bowl; beat at medium speed with an electric mixer until mixture is smooth. Cover "Sponge" and let rise in a warm place (85 degrees F) free from drafts, 30 minutes or until doubled in size.

Makes 1 ½ cups

EASY DINNER ROLLS

2 ½ teaspoons dry yeast

1 cup (250ml) milk

4 Tablespoons butter

2 Tablespoons sugar

2 eggs, beaten

4 cups (560g) unbleached flour

2 teaspoons salt

2 Tablespoons melted butter to glaze, plus extra to grease bowl and baking sheet

Directions

1. Sprinkle the yeast into ½ cup (125ml) of milk in a bowl. Leave 5 minutes; stir to dissolve. Warm the remaining milk in a saucepan with the butter and sugar. Stir until butter has melted. Cool until lukewarm, and then beat in the eggs until evenly blended.

2. Mix the flour and salt in a large bowl. Make a well in the center and pour in the dissolved yeast and butter mixture. Mix the flour to form soft sticky dough.

3. Turn the dough out onto a floured surface. Knead until smooth, shiny, and elastic, about 10 minutes. Kneed in extra flour; 1 Tablespoon at a time, if dough is too sticky. Resist adding too much flour, as dough should not be dry, but soft.

4. Place the dough in a buttered bowl. Let rise until doubled in size, 1-1 ½ hours. Punch down, let rest for 10 minutes.

5. Divide the dough into two pieces. Roll out each piece to form an 8in x 16in (20cm x 40cm) rectangle. Cut each rectangle lengthwise into four strips each 2in (5cm) wide. Cut each strip into four rectangles, each 4in (10cm) long. Brush ½ of each rectangle with melted butter, and then fold in half, leaving a ½ in (1cm) flap.

6. Place the rolls on a buttered baking sheet so each roll overlaps slightly with the one next to it; cover with a dish towel. Proof until doubled in size, about 10 minutes.

7. Brush the tops of the rolls with melted butter. Bake in preheated oven 425 degrees F (220 C) for 15 to 20 minutes. Until golden and hollow sounding when tapped underneath. Cool on wire rack.

ALMOND-ANISE BISCOTTI

½ cup butter or margarine

¼ cup canola or vegetable oil

1 ¼ cups sugar

6 large eggs

1 teaspoon anise oil

1 ½ teaspoons vanilla

6 to 7 cups all-purpose flour, divided

1 teaspoon baking powder

2 cups whole blanched almonds

1 ½ cups sifted powdered sugar

2 Tablespoons milk

Chopped almonds or sugar, if desired

Directions

1. Beat butter, oil and sugar with an electric mixer at medium speed until well blended. Add eggs, one at a time, beating after each addition. Stir in anise oil and vanilla.

2. Combine 6 cups flour and baking powder; add butter mixture. Gradually add enough remaining flour to make stiff dough. Stir in almonds, lightly flour hands, and divide dough into 5 portions.

Shape each portion into 8-inch long log, and place on lightly greased cookie sheet; Bake at 350 degrees F. for 35 minutes or until lightly browned; cool on wire rack

3. Using a serrated knife carefully cut each log crosswise into ½ - inch slices. Place on ungreased cookie sheet; bake at 350 degrees F. for 10 minutes on each side. Cool on wire racks

4. Combine powdered sugar and milk; spread over top of each biscotti, and sprinkle with chopped almonds or sugar, if desired

Makes about 5 ½ dozen

ORANGE-CRANBERRY BREAD

This recipe is so delicious, fluffy and yummy, also makes a great gift from your kitchen. If you prefer use orange juice instead of the Grand Marnier its will still be just as yummy.

1½ cups unsalted butter, softened: plus extra to butter pans.

1½ cups sugar

4 eggs

1 cup orange juice

1 cup sour cream

2 Tablespoons freshly grated orange zest

2 teaspoons vanilla extract

4 cups all-purpose flour

1 Tablespoon baking powder

½ teaspoon salt

1½ cups dried cranberries

2 cups powdered sugar

8 Tablespoons Grand Marnier or other orange liqueur

Directions

1. Preheat oven to 350 degrees F. Butter two 9 x 5-inch loaf pans (or if making the mini loaves, butter six mini loaf pans).

2. With an electric mixer, cream butter and sugar together, on medium speed until pale and fluffy, about 3 minutes. Add eggs one at a time, mixing well after each. Add orange juice, sour cream, orange zest, and vanilla; mix until blended.

3. In a separate bowl, whisk together flour, baking powder, and salt. Add flour mixture and cranberries to butter mixture and mix just until dry ingredients are just moistened; do not over mix.

4. Pour batter into prepared loaf pans. Bake for 70 to 75 minutes for large loaves and 60 minutes for mini loaves, or until toothpick inserted in center comes out clean.

5. In a small bowl, combine powdered sugar and 7 Tablespoons Grand Marnier. Glaze should have consistency of thick maple syrup or corn syrup. If it is too thick, add additional Tablespoon liqueur.

6. Let loaves cool in pans for 10 minutes, then remove and transfer to wire rack set over a large baking sheet. With a thin skewer or long toothpick, poke deep holes in tops of loaves. Drizzle with Grand Marnier glaze so that it coats the top, runs down the sides, and seeps through the holes.

7. Let loaves cool completely, then slice and serve, or wrap and freeze. Makes two loaves (9x5-inch)

Make Ahead Recipe: Make loaves up to 1 month ahead and freeze. Bake and glaze loaves and allow them to cool completely. Wrap tightly with plastic wrap, put in resealable plastic bags, and freeze. When ready to serve, remove from freezer and defrost at room temperature.

BANANA-CHOCOLATE CHIP BREAD

½ cup butter softened

½ cup sugar

2 eggs

3 bananas mashed

2 cups all-purpose flour

1 teaspoon baking soda

½ cup honey-roasted peanuts, chopped

½ cup semisweet chocolate chips.

Directions

1. Preheat oven to 350 degrees F. Grease and flour a 9 x 5 loaf pan.

2. In a large bowl combine all ingredients; mix well and pour into prepared pan. Bake for 1 hour. Allow to cool for 15 minutes in pan Transfer to a wire rack to cool.

CRANBERRY APPLE CRISP

5 cups tart apples (about 6 medium apples), pared and sliced

1½ cups fresh or frozen cranberries

1/3 cup sugar

½ cup all-purpose flour

½ cup brown sugar

1 teaspoon cinnamon

¼ cup butter

Directions

1. Preheat oven to 375 degrees F. Lightly grease a 9-inch square baking pan.

2. Layer apples and cranberries in pan, sprinkling with sugar as you layer

3. Make topping: Mix flour, brown sugar, and cinnamon. Blend in butter with fingertips or pastry blender until light and crumbly. Sprinkle topping evenly over apples and cranberries. Bake 45 minutes or until apples are tender.

Makes 9 Servings

FROZEN PUMPKIN DESSERT

¾ cup graham cracker crumbs

¼ cup sugar

3 Tablespoons margarine or butter, melted

Vegetable cooking spray

1 ½ cups canned pumpkin

¾ cup sifted powdered sugar

1 teaspoon ground cinnamon

¼ teaspoon ground cloves

¼ teaspoon ground nutmeg

¼ teaspoon salt

4 cups nonfat frozen dessert, softened

2 Tablespoons graham cracker crumbs

Directions

1. Combine first 3 ingredients, stirring well. Press mixture into bottom of an 11x7x1 ½ -inch baking dish coated with cooking spray. Bake at 350 degrees F. for 8 minutes. Let cool completely on wire rack.

2. Combine pumpkin, powdered sugar, cinnamon, cloves, nutmeg and salt in a large bowl; Stirring well. Add frozen dessert, with an electric mixer; beat on low speed for 1 minute or until smooth.

3. Spoon into prepared dish. Sprinkle 2 Tablespoons graham cracker crumbs over pumpkin mixture. Cover and freeze until firm.

Makes 10 servings

SWEET ROLL PUDDING

1 (7-oz) can refrigerated cinnamon raisin rolls

2 large eggs

1½ cups milk

¾ cup sugar

1 teaspoon vanilla extract

¼ cup butter

2 Tablespoons honey

Directions

1. Bake rolls according to package directions; cool and crumble. Sprinkle 3 cups crumbs into lightly greased 1½ -quart baking dish.

2. Combine eggs and milk; stir in eggs and vanilla, and pour over crumbs.

3. Combine butter and honey; pour over egg mixture.

4. Bake at 300 degrees F. for 1 hour or until golden.

Makes 4 to 6 Servings

STEAMED HOLIDAY PUDDING

Steamed puddings are a long standing holiday tradition, if you have never made on I have a couple for you. Even through many ingredients are used these puddings they are simple to prepare. You will get better results if a steamed pudding mold with a locking top is used... However you can use heat-proof bowls, covered with a double thickness of buttered aluminum foil secured with string.

2 1/3 cups all-purpose flour

1 1/3 cups finely chopped suet

1 1/3 cups firmly packed brown sugar

½ teaspoon salt

½ teaspoon ground cinnamon

¼ teaspoon ground cloves

¼ teaspoon ground ginger

¼ teaspoon ground nutmeg

2 eggs, well beaten

2/3 cup orange juice

2/3 cup water

1 1/3 cups chopped raisins

1 1/3 cups chopped mixed candid fruit

1 1/3 cups currants

2/3 cup finely chopped figs

Commercial hard sauce

Directions

In a large bowl, combine first 8 ingredients; mix well. Add eggs, orange juice and water; stir well. Combine raisins, candied fruit, currants and figs; add to flour mixture, stirring well. Spoon mixture into greased; 1 ½-quart steamed pudding mold; cover tightly.

2. Place mold on a shallow rack in a large, deep kettle with enough boiling water to come two-thirds up the mold. Cover kettle; steam pudding about 5 hours in continuously boiling water. (Replace water as needed). Let pudding stand 5 minutes; unmold and serve with hard sauce.

Makes 10 to 12 servings

FLAMED PLUM PUDDING

½ cup butter, softened

1 ½ cups firmly packed brown sugar

2 eggs beaten

1 teaspoon vanilla extract

1 cup scraped, grated carrots

1 cup raisins

1 cup dried figs, chopped

1 cup pecans, chopped

½ cup currants

1 cup all-purpose flour

1 teaspoon baking soda

½ teaspoon salt

1 teaspoon ground cinnamon

1 teaspoon ground ginger

½ teaspoon ground allspice

¼ teaspoon ground nutmeg

1 cup fine, dry breadcrumbs

1/8 cup brandy

1/8 cup sherry

¼ cup plus 2 Tablespoons brandy, divided

Directions

1. Cream butter; gradually add sugar, beating well. Add eggs and vanilla; beat well. Stir in next 5 ingredients, mixing well. Combine flour, soda, salt and spices; add to creamed mixture. Stir in breadcrumbs, 1/8 cup brandy and sherry. Stir until all ingredients are combined.

2. Spoon mixture into a well-greased 1 ½ -quart steamed pudding mold; cover mold tightly.

3. Place mold on a shallow rack in a large deep kettle with enough boiling water to come halfway up mold. Cover kettle; steam pudding 3 hours in continuously boiling water. (Replace water as needed).

4. Let pudding stand 5 minutes; unmold onto serving plate. Pour 2 Tablespoons brandy over hot pudding. Heat remaining ¼ cup brandy in a small saucepan to produce fumes (Do Not Boil): ignite and pour over pudding. Chill overnight.

Makes 10 to 12 Servings

CHERRIES JUBILEE

½ cup white sugar

2 tablespoon cornstarch

1/3 c water

1/4 c orange juice

1(48-oz.) bag of frozen pitted cherries

1 (10-oz) jar or can (1-cup) of Bing cherries

½ teaspoon finely grated orange zest

¼ cup brandy

Premium vanilla ice cream

Directions

1. Whisk together the sugar and cornstarch, water and orange juice in a wide saucepan. Bring to a boil over medium heat, whisking until thickened. Stir in the cherries and orange zest and bring to boil. Reduce heat, and simmer for 10 minutes.

2. While the cherries are cooking, spoon the ice cream into serving bowls. Remove the cherries from the burner, stir in the brandy, and ignite with a long lighter. Gently shake the pan until the blue flame has extinguished itself. Spoon the cherries over the bowls of ice cream.

Makes 6 to 8 servings

This sweet cheery cherry chewy treat, Is great for holiday entertaining

6 cups sweetened flaked coconut

2 large eggs

1 (14-oz.) can sweetened condensed milk

½ teaspoon vanilla extract

1 teaspoon cherry extract

1 cup chopped Maraschino cherries

Directions

1. Preheat oven at 350 degrees F. Line baking sheets with parchment paper.

2. In a large mixing bowl, place the sweetened flaked coconut. In another bowl, whisk the sweetened condensed milk, eggs, vanilla extract and cherry extract; mix well. Add the milk mixture into the flaked coconut. Then stir in the chopped maraschino cherries.

3. Using a teaspoon, form small mounds/balls of the macaroon mixture and place each onto parchment lined cookie sheets.

4. Bake in a 350'F preheated oven for 15 minutes or until top and bottom turned slightly golden brown.

Store macaroons flat separating each layer with parchment paper. Keep in an airtight container. Makes about 40 Macaroons

LEMON FILLED MACAROONS

3 large egg yolks

½ cup powdered sugar

¼ cup fresh lemon juice

1 ½ teaspoons finely grated lemon zest

4 Tablespoons unsalted butter, at room temperature

Macaroons

1 2/3 cups sifted confectioners' sugar

1 cup blanched almonds (5½-oz)

¾ teaspoon whole pink peppercorns

3 large egg whites, at room temperature

¾ cup granulated sugar

¼ cup water

Directions

1. Preheat the oven to 350° and line 2 baking sheets with parchment paper.

2. Make the lemon filling: In the top of a double boiler filled with 2 inches of simmering water, combine the egg yolks, powdered sugar, lemon juice and zest. Cook over moderately low heat, whisking constantly, until thickened and an instant-read thermometer inserted in the curd registers 180°, about 10 minutes. Remove from the heat and whisk in the butter. Strain the curd into a heatproof bowl. Press plastic wrap directly onto the surface and refrigerate until chilled.

3. Make the Macaroons: In a food processor, combine the powdered sugar, almonds and pink peppercorns and process until

powdery. Transfer the mixture to a large bowl and break up any lumps.

4. In the bowl of a standing electric mixer fitted with the whisk, or large bowl using an electric hand mixer; beat 2 of the egg whites at high speed until soft peaks form. Turn the mixer to the lowest setting while the sugar syrup cooks. In a small saucepan, combine the granulated sugar with the water and cook until the syrup reaches 238° on an instant-read thermometer, about 5 minutes. Increase the speed to moderately high and carefully and slowly pour the hot sugar syrup into the beaten whites in a thin stream. Beat until the meringue is stiff and glossy, about 5 minutes.

5. Pour the remaining egg white over the almond mixture and scrape the meringue on top. Using a rubber spatula, fold everything together until completely combined. Transfer the meringue to a pastry bag fitted with a ½-inch plain tip. Pipe 1-inch mounds of meringue onto the prepared baking sheets, about 1 inch apart. Give each baking sheet a firm tap on the table to release any air bubbles. Rotate the pans and tap again. Using slightly moistened fingertips, press the meringues so they are about ¼-inch high. Let stand at room temperature for 30 minutes to allow the tops to dry.

6. Bake 1 sheet at a time in the center of the oven for 10 minutes, until the meringues are lightly browned. Let cool completely on the baking sheet, then carefully lift off the macaroons.

7. Scrape the lemon filling into a pastry bag fitted with a ¼- inch plain tip. Pipe the lemon curd onto the flat side of half of the macaroons and top them with the remaining cookies. Pipe a tiny dot of lemon filling on top of each one. Makes 42 macaroons

Tip: The lemon curd can be refrigerated for up to 4 days.

CHOCOLATE COOKIES

Very rich and chocolaty-chewy and soft; for the chocolate lovers

10 ounce bittersweet chocolate, chopped

2 ounces unsweetened chocolate, chopped

¼ cup unsalted butter, cut into chunks

3 large eggs, at room temperature

1 cup sugar

¾ cup flour

¾ teaspoon baking powder

¼ teaspoon kosher salt

Directions

1. Place chocolates and butter in a medium metal bowl and set bowl over a pan filled with 1 in. of simmering water. Cook, stirring occasionally, until melted, then remove from heat and let cool slightly. Whisk in eggs and sugar, mixing until combined. Then whisk in flour, baking powder, and salt. Chill dough, covered, until firm, about 2 hours.

2. Let dough sit at room temperature 15 minutes. Meanwhile, preheat oven to 350 degrees F. and line 2 baking sheets with parchment paper. Scoop 1 Tablespoon portions of dough; rolling each into a ball, and put onto baking sheets 1 in. apart. Bake cookies until they no longer look wet on top, about 8 minutes. Let cool on baking sheets.

Make ahead: Batter up to 1 day; baked cookies up to 2 days, airtight. Makes about 40 cookies

A glass of cold milk and freshly baked chocolate peppermint cookies makes an unbeatable afternoon snack.

½ cup margarine, or butter, softened

½ cup sugar

½ cup firmly packed brown sugar

½ cup frozen egg substitute, thawed

1 teaspoon vanilla extract

2 ¼ cups all-purpose flour

1 teaspoon baking powder

¼ teaspoon baking soda

¼ teaspoon salt

¼ cup plus 1 Tablespoon unsweetened cocoa

2/3 cup finely crushed peppermint candies (about 30 candies)

Vegetable cooking spray

Directions

1. Beat margarine with an electric mixer at medium speed until creamy; gradually add white and brown sugars, beating well. Add egg substitute and vanilla; beat well.

2. Combine flour, baking powder, baking soda, salt and cocoa. Add to margarine mixture, stirring until just blended. Stir in crushed candy. Drop dough by level Tablespoonful's, 2-inches apart, on cookie sheets sprayed with vegetable spray.

3. Bake at 350 degrees F for 10 to 12 minutes. Remove from cookie sheets, let cool on wire racks

Makes 44 cookies

ZUCCHINI-CHOCOLATE BROWNIES

Enjoy your veggies with desserts

2 cups zucchini, grated

½ cup virgin coconut oil

½ cup honey

2 eggs

1 teaspoon vanilla extract

1¾ cups whole wheat pastry flour

1/2 cup unsweetened cocoa powder

1/2 teaspoon salt

1 1/2 teaspoon baking powder

1/2 teaspoon cinnamon

1 1/2 cups (12 ounces) semi-sweet or dark chocolate chips

Directions

1. Preheat oven to 350 degrees and grease an 8 inch square baking pan.

Grate zucchini. Dump into a mesh colander and squeeze it with a towel to get rid of excess moisture. Fluff it back up with a fork.

2. In a large bowl, beat together the wet ingredients (oil, eggs, honey and vanilla). Stir in the zucchini. In a separate, smaller bowl,

stir together the dry ingredients (whole wheat pastry flour, cocoa, salt, baking powder and cinnamon).Pour the dry mixture into the wet/zucchini mixture. Stir just until combined, and then stir in the chocolate chips. Pour the batter into your prepared pan.

3. Bake 30-35 minutes or until a toothpick inserted in the center comes out clean. Let cool completely.

GRANOLA MERINGUE COOKIES

Store these sweet treats in an air tight container to keep then crisp.

3 egg whites

½ teaspoon cream of tartar

¼ cup plus 2 Tablespoons sugar

¾ cup granola cereal without raisins

¼ teaspoon vanilla extract

¼ teaspoon almond extract

Directions

1. Line 2 baking sheets with parchment paper; set aside

2. Beat eggs whites and cream of tartar; with an electric mixer on high speed until foamy. Gradually add sugar, 1 Tablespoon at a time, beating until stiff peaks form and sugar dissolves (2 to 4 minutes) Fold in cereal, vanilla and almond extracts.

3. Drop mixture by level Tablespoonful 2 inches apart onto prepared baking sheets. Bake at 225 degrees F. for 1 hour and 10 minutes. Turn oven off. Cool in oven for 2 hours with the oven door closed. Carefully remove cookies from paper; let cool completely on wire racks. Makes 4 dozen cookies

CROWN ROAST WITH CRANBERRY-PECAN STUFFING

1 Tablespoon salt

1 Tablespoon black pepper

2 teaspoons dried thyme

1 (16-rib) crown pork roast, trimmed

2 cups Cranberry-pecan Stuffing

¼ cup butter or margarine

1/3 cup all-purpose flour

2 (14 ½ -oz.) cans chicken broth

2 Tablespoons orange liqueur

2 Tablespoons grated orange peel

¼ teaspoon salt

¼ teaspoon pepper

Garnishes: Kumquat leaves, sugared kumquats, grape clusters, or crab apples, if desired

Directions

1. Combine first 3 ingredients; rub over all sides of roast.

2. Fold a piece of foil into an 8-inch square; place on a rack in a roasting pan. Place roast, bone ends up, on foil lined rack.3. Bake at 350 degrees F. for 1 hour.

4. Spoon 2 cups Cranberry-Pecan Stuffing into the center of the roast; cover with a 12-inch square of heavy-duty foil, and fold over tips of ribs.

5. Bake at 350 degrees F, for 1 ½ hours or until a meat thermometer registers 160 degrees F. Remove foil; let stand 15 minutes before slicing.

6. Pour pan drippings into a skillet; add butter and cook over medium heat until butter melts. Add flour, whisking until smooth; cook whisking constantly, until caramel colored.

7. Stir in chicken broth and next 4 ingredients; cook, whisking constantly; until smooth and thickened. Serve with roast. Garnish if desired

Makes 12 Servings

This stuffing can be made the day before. Just; place in a large bowl and refrigerate until ready to bake, if not preparing a roast, spoon all the stuffing; Into 2 lightly greased 11x7x1½ –inch baking pans, bake as directed.

2 cups dried cranberries

1 cup orange liqueur

2 pounds mild ground pork sausage

4 cups coarsely chopped celery

1 ½ cups chopped onion

½ cup butter or margarine

1 (14 ½ -oz.) can chicken broth

1 teaspoon salt

½ teaspoon pepper

1 teaspoon thyme

2 (16-oz) pkg. Pork stuffing mix

2 Tablespoons grated orange peel

2 cups chopped pecans

Directions

1. In a small saucepan, combine cranberries and liqueur; bring to a boil over medium-high heat. Remove from heat, set aside.

2. In a large skillet, brown sausage, stirring until it crumbles; drain, reserving 2 Tablespoons drippings in skillet. Set aside.

3. Add celery and onions to reserved drippings; cook over medium high heat 10 minutes, stirring constantly. Add butter, chicken broth, salt, pepper and thyme; cook stirring constantly, 3 minutes or until butter melts.

4. In a large bowl, combine cranberry mixture, sausage and stuffing mix and seasoning packets, orange peel and pecans, stir well.

5. Spoon 2 cups stuffing into the center of crown pork roast: spoon remaining stuffing into lightly greased 13 x 9 x 2-inch baking pan.

6. Cover and bake at 350 degrees F. for 20 minutes; uncover and bake 10 additional minutes or until lightly browned.

Makes 12 Servings

1 (4-pound) cleaned duckling (fresh or frozen) thawed

1 ½ Tablespoons five-spice seasoning powder

1 teaspoon salt

4 cups rock salt

Directions

1. Preheat oven to 500 degrees F.

2. Remove giblets and neck from duckling; reserve for another use. Rinse duckling under cold water; pat dry. Trim excess fat. Starting at neck cavity; loosen skin from breast and drumsticks, by inserting fingers and pushing hand between skin and meat.

3. Combine five-spice powder and 1 teaspoon salt. Sprinkle spice mixture under loosened skin; rub into body cavity. Tie ends of legs together with string. Lift wing tips up and over back; tuck under duckling.

4. Spread rock salt in bottom of a shallow roasting pan. Place duckling, breast side up, on rock salt. Pierce skin several times with a meat fork. Insert a meat thermometer into meaty part of thigh; make sure not to touch bone.

5. Bake in preheated oven for 45 minutes or until thermometer registers 180 degrees F. Cover loosely with foil; let stand 10 minutes. Discard skin. Makes 4 (3-oz) servings

TURKEY IN A BAG

10 to 12 pounds whole turkey

Salt and pepper to taste

1 Tablespoon thyme

2 teaspoons rosemary, crushed

1 teaspoon rubbed sage, optional

2 Tablespoons butter

Olive oil cooking spray

2 tablespoons all-purpose flour

5 stalks celery

2 large onions, quartered

Directions

1. Preheat oven to 350 degrees F.

2. Rinse turkey and remove giblets.

3. Season cavity with, thyme, rosemary, sage, salt and pepper to taste. With fingers loosen skin from breast meat, Press slices of cold butter between skin and breast meat. Spray skin with olive oil spray, if desired

Sprinkle the bottom of a turkey size oven bag with flour. Place turkey, celery and onions in the bag. Seal bag, with a fork piece several holes in bag.

4. Bake 3 to 3 ½ hours, or until internal temperature of the thigh meat reaches 180 degrees F. Let stand 20 minutes before carving.

1 ¼ pounds giblets and neck from turkey

1 cup chopped onion

1 cup chopped celery

1 cup chopped carrots

1 pinch ground black pepper, or to taste

2 (1.2 ounce) packages dry turkey gravy mix

3 (14.5 ounce) cans chicken broth, or more as needed

2 cups turkey drippings

1/4 cup quick-mixing flour (such as Wondra)

Directions

1. Place the giblets and turkey neck into a large saucepan with onion, celery, carrots, pepper, and turkey gravy mix. Pour the chicken broth over the mixture, bring to a simmer over medium-low heat, and simmer for 40 minutes. Remove the turkey liver and set aside. Allow the stock to simmer for 2 more hours. Stock should equal about 3 cups; add more chicken broth if necessary. Remove the giblets and chop, chop the liver if desired; set aside, Strain the stock into a saucepan; discard bones and vegetables.

2. When the turkey is finished roasting, pour the drippings into a fat separator or bowl, and skim off the fat. In a bowl, whisk the quick-mixing flour with the pan drippings until smooth, and then whisk the flour mixture into the stock. Bring the gravy mixture to a simmer over medium heat, whisking constantly, and add the chopped giblets, if desired.

Makes about 5 cups

TURKEY BREAST STUFFED WITH WILD RICE & CRANBERRIES

4 cups cooked wild rice

¾ cup onion, finely chopped

½ cup dried cranberries

1/3 cup slivered almonds

2 medium golden delicious apples, peeled or unpeeled, coarsely chopped (2 cups)

1 boneless whole turkey breast (4 to 5 lbs.) thawed if frozen.

Directions

1. In a medium bowl, mix all ingredients except turkey. Cut turkey into slices at 1-inch intervals about ¾ the way through, forming deep pockets.

2. Place turkey in 3 ½ quart or larger slow cooker. Stuff pockets with wild rice mixture. Place remaining rice mixture around edges of cooker.

3. Cover and cook on Low 8 to 10 hours, until turkey is no longer pink inside.

Makes 10 Servings

½ cup chopped celery, including tops

1 medium onion, chopped

¼ cup butter (½ stick)

6 cups dry bread crumbs

1 large sweet potato, cooked, peeled, finely chopped

½ cup chicken broth

¼ cup chopped toasted pecans

½ teaspoon poultry seasoning

¼ teaspoon rubbed sage

½ teaspoon salt

¼ teaspoon black or white pepper

Directions

In heavy skillet, melt butter over medium heat; sauté celery and onion until tender, stirring frequently. Add remaining ingredients and toss gently to coat. Grease a 4 to 5 quart and fill with stuffing, ½ to ¾ full. Cover crock-pot and cook on Low for 4-5 hours until stuffing is hot.

Makes 6-8 Servings

SLOW-COOKER TURKEY

3 celery stalks, chopped

1 small onion, chopped

3 garlic cloves, minced

½ cup chicken broth

1 (6 -7 lbs.) bone-in turkey breast

1 (1 ounce) envelope dry onion soup mix

1 Tablespoon butter

Directions

1. Place celery, onion, minced garlic and chicken broth on bottom of slow cooker.

2. Rinse the turkey breast and pat dry. Cut off any excess skin, but leave the skin covering the breast. Rub onion soup mix all over outside and lifting the skin, directly on the meat of the turkey.

3. Place in a slow cooker, drizzle with 1 Tablespoon butter; Cover, and cook on High for 1 hour, then set to Low, and cook for 7 hours.

2 Cornish Game Hens, about 1-½ pounds each

1 Tablespoon chopped Fresh Rosemary

1 Tablespoon chopped Fresh Tarragon

1 Tablespoon chopped Fresh Parsley

1 Tablespoon grated orange or lemon zest

2 garlic cloves, minced

1 Tablespoon Olive Oil

½ teaspoon salt

¼ teaspoon ground black pepper

Directions:

1. Preheat oven to 400 degrees. Using kitchen shears, cut along each side of the backbone of hens; discard backbones. Turn hens, breast side up and open flat. Using the palm of your hand, flatten breasts slightly so the halves lay flat. With your fingers, carefully loosen the skin under the breasts, legs, and thighs.

2. In a small bowl, stir together all remaining ingredients. Rub the herb mixture on meat under loosened skin; press skin back in place. Tuck the wings under hens.

3. Spray a large ovenproof skillet with nonstick spray and set over medium-high heat. Add hens, breast side down and cook until browned, about 5 minutes, without turning. Place a piece of foil on top of hens, and then place a cast-iron skillet on top of foil, pressing down on chicken.

4. Place pan in oven and roast hens for 25 minutes. Remove cast iron skillet and foil from pan. Carefully turn hens over and roast, uncovered, an additional 10 minutes. Let hens rest for 10 minutes before serving. Cut each hen in half to make 4 servings

4 small Cornish game hens

1 carrot, finely diced

1 stalk celery, finely diced

2 cups bread stuffing mix

1 teaspoon poultry seasoning

1 cup chicken stock or broth

Salt and pepper

Sauce

1 cup fresh or frozen cranberries, chopped

1 (12-oz) jar, sweet orange marmalade

¼ cup water

1 teaspoon lemon juice

Lemon wedges, optional

Directions

1. Preheat oven to 400 degrees F. Trim as much fat as possible from game hens. Combine carrots, celery, stuffing mix, poultry seasoning and chicken stock, Season stuffing with salt and pepper, to taste. Fill cavity of each game hen with stuffing; Bake for 45 minutes.

2. Meanwhile, prepare sauce. In a medium saucepan, combine all ingredients. Cook over medium heat for 5 to 8 minutes or until cranberries have released their juice; set aside.

3. Remove game hens from oven. Spread sauce over top and sides of hens. Reserve any extra sauce to serve later with hens. Return hens to oven and continue baking 10 to 15 minutes.

To Serve: Place game hens on 4 serving plates. Spoon some onto each plate. Spoon additional sauce over hens Garnish with lemon wedges, if desired.

Makes 4 servings

ROAST LEMON-HERB CHICKEN

1 (5 to 6-pound) roasting chicken

Kosher salt

Freshly ground black pepper

1 large bunch fresh thyme

4 or 5 Sprigs rosemary

4 lemons

3 heads garlic, cut in 1/2 crosswise

2 tablespoons butter, melted

1/2 pound sliced bacon

1 cup white wine

1/2 cup chicken stock

Directions

1. Preheat the oven to 425 degrees F.2. Remove the chicken giblets. Rinse the chicken inside and out. Remove any excess fat and leftover pinfeathers and pat the outside dry. Place the chicken in a large roasting pan. Liberally salt and pepper the inside of the chicken. Stuff the cavity with the rosemary and thyme, reserving enough thyme to garnish the chicken dish, 1 lemon, halved, and 2 halves of the garlic. Brush the outside of the chicken with the butter and sprinkle again with salt and pepper. Tie the legs together with kitchen string and tuck the wing tips under the body of the chicken. Cut 2 of the lemons in quarters and scatter the quarters and remaining garlic around the chicken. Lay the bacon slices over the chicken to cover.

3. Roast the chicken for 1 hour. Remove the bacon slices from the top of the chicken and set aside. Continue roasting the chicken for an additional 30 minutes, or until the juices run clear when you cut between a leg and thigh. Remove to a platter and cover with aluminum foil while you prepare the gravy.

4. Remove all but 4 tablespoons of the fat and juices from the bottom of the pan. Add the wine and chicken stock and bring it to a boil. Reduce the heat, and simmer for 5 minutes, or until reduced by half.

4. Slice the chicken on a platter. Garnish the chicken platter with the bacon slices, roasted garlic, reserved thyme and 1 lemon, sliced. Serve with the gravy.

LEMON CHICKEN WITH BOK CHOY

When buying Bok Choy, choose stalks that are pure white and firm and look for dark green leaves.

4 chicken breast halves, boneless and skinless, pounded to 1/3" thickness

3 eggs

½ cup flour

½ cup plus 2 teaspoons cornstarch, divided

½ cup canola oil

6 stalks bok Choy

½ cup lemon juice

1 Tablespoon white wine vinegar

1/3 cup plus 1 Tablespoon sugar

1/4 cup plus 2 tablespoons water, divided

Directions

1. Preheat oven to 200 degrees F. Line baking sheet with paper towels.

2. In shallow bowl, whisk eggs. In glass pie dish or other shallow baking dish, combine flour and ½ cup cornstarch. Dip chicken into

beaten eggs; drain off excess. Toss chicken in flour-cornstarch mixture and coat well. Transfer chicken to plate and set aside.

3. In straight-sided sauté pan, warm canola oil. Add chicken to pan, in batches if necessary, and fry until golden brown, crispy and cooked through, about 7 to 8 minutes. Transfer chicken to prepared baking sheet; place in warmed oven.

3. Prepare bok Choy by steaming over boiling water about 3 to 4 minutes.

4. Make lemon sauce: In a small saucepan combine lemon juice, vinegar, sugar and ¼ cup water. Place over low heat and cook, stirring, until the sugar is dissolved, about 2 to 3 minutes. Increase heat to medium-high and bring to a boil. Reduce heat to low and simmer 1 to 2 minutes. In small bowl, whisk together 2 teaspoons cornstarch and 2 Tablespoons water. Whisk cornstarch mixture into the sauce; cook until sauce boils and thickens about 2 to 3 minutes.

3. In large fry pan over medium heat, warm lemon sauce. Add chicken; turn to coat lightly with the sauce. Transfer chicken to cutting board and cut into 1/2-inch slices.

Place Bok Choy stalks on platter. Place chicken pieces on top of Bok Choy; drizzle remaining sauce over chicken.

Makes 4 servings

HERB ROASTED RACK OF LAMB

½ cup mango chutney, chopped

2 to 3 garlic cloves, minced

2 whole racks (6 ribs each) lamb loin chops

1 cup fresh French or Italian bread crumbs

1 Tablespoon chopped fresh thyme or 1 teaspoon dried thyme

1 Tablespoon chopped fresh rosemary or 1 teaspoon dried Rosemary

1 Tablespoon chopped fresh oregano or 1 teaspoon dried oregano

Directions

1. Preheat oven to 400 degrees F. In a small bowl, combine chutney and garlic; spread evenly over meaty side of lamb with a thin spatula... Combine remaining ingredients in a small bowl; pat crumb mixture evenly over chutney mixture.

2. Place lamb racks, crumb side up, on rack in shallow roasting pan. Roast in oven about 30 minutes or until instant read thermometer inserted into lamb, but not touching bone, registers 145 degrees F. for medium or to desired doneness.

3. Place lamb in carving board; tent with foil. Let stand 10 minutes for easier slicing. Internal temperature will continue to rise about 5 to 10 degrees during stand time. Slice between ribs into individual chops with large carving knife. Garnish with additional fresh herbs and mango slices, if desired. Serve immediately.

Makes 4 Servings

Horseradish Cream Sauce

3 garlic cloves, minced

1 teaspoon black pepper

3 rib standing roast, trimmed, (6 to7 lbs.)

Directions

1. Prepare Horseradish Cream Sauce. Preheat oven to 450 degrees F. Combine garlic and pepper, rub over surface of roast.

2. Place roast bone side down in shallow roasting pan. Insert meat thermometer in thickest part of roast, not touching bone or fat. Roast 15 minutes.

3. Reduce oven temperature to 325 degrees F. Roast 20 minutes per pound or until internal temperature is 145 degrees F. for medium.

4. When roast has reached desired temperature; transfer to cutting board; tent with foil, let stand 15 to 20 minutes to allow for easier carving. Temperature of roast will continue to rise about 10 degrees F. during standing time. Serve with Horseradish Cream Sauce. Makes 8 Servings

HORSERADISH CREAM SAUCE

1 cup whipping cream

¼ cup prepared horseradish, undrained

2 teaspoons balsamic or red wine vinegar

1 teaspoon dry mustard

¼ teaspoon sugar

1/8 teaspoon salt

Directions

Beat cream until soft peaks form. Do not overbeat. In a medium bowl; combine horseradish, vinegar, mustard, sugar and salt. Fold whipped cream into horseradish mixture. Cover and refrigerate at least 1 hour. Sauce may be made up to 8 hours before serving

Makes 1 ½ cups

Note: For extra flavor, rub with fresh herbs, such as chopped thyme leaves and rosemary, onto the meat before roasting.

14-16 pound Boneless Ham Roast

3 Tablespoons Salt

1 cup Chicken Broth

½ cup Creamy Peanut Butter

3 Tablespoons Maple Syrup

2 garlic cloves, minced

½ teaspoon Worcestershire Sauce

3 Chipotle Peppers In Adobo, finely minced

Directions

Preheat oven to 300 degrees. Salt ham all over: Place in large baking dish in oven and bake for 4 ½ hours. In a food processor, combine the chicken broth, peanut butter, maple syrup, garlic, Worcestershire sauce, and chipotles in adobo. Forty minutes before the ham is done, remove from oven, pour sauce all over, and return to oven to finish baking. Allow ham to rest for 15 minutes before carving.

STEAK WITH GARLIC BUTTER

6 medium cloves garlic

Kosher salt

1½ pounds skirt steak, trimmed and cut into 4 pieces

Freshly ground black pepper

2 Tbs. canola oil or vegetable oil

2 oz. (4 Tbs.) unsalted butter

1 Tbs. chopped fresh flat-leaf parsley

Directions

1. Peel the garlic cloves and smash them with the side of a chef's knife. Sprinkle the garlic lightly with salt and mince it.

2. Pat the steak dry and season generously on both sides with salt and pepper. In a heavy-duty 12-inch skillet, heat the oil over medium-high heat until shimmering hot. Add the steak and brown well on both sides, 2 to 3 minutes per side for medium rare. Transfer the steak to a plate and let rest while you make the garlic butter.

3. In an 8-inch skillet, melt the butter over low heat. Add the garlic and cook, swirling the pan frequently, until lightly golden, about 4 minutes. Lightly salt to taste

4. Slice the steak, if desired, and transfer to 4 plates. Spoon the garlic butter over the steak, sprinkle with the parsley, and serve.

Makes 4 servings

TANGERINE SWEET POTATOES

9 cups peeled, thinly sliced sweet potatoes (about 2 ½ lbs.)

8 lemon slices

Vegetable cooking spray

2/3 cup firmly packed brown sugar

1 Tablespoon grated tangerine or orange peel

½ cup fresh tangerine or orange juice

2 Tablespoons margarine, butter or coconut oil, melted

Directions

1. Preheat oven to 400 degrees F. Spray 13 x 9-inch baking dish with vegetable cooking spray.

2. Arrange sweet potatoes and lemon slices in prepared baking dish. Combine brown sugar, grated tangerine peel, tangerine juice and margarine. Drizzle sugar mixture over sweet potatoes; cover with foil. Bake for 35 minutes. Uncover potatoes and stir well; bake an additional 30 minutes.

Makes 12 ½ cup Servings

TWICE BAKED SWEET POTATOES

A variation on twice-baked potatoes, these are an eye-catching takeoff on a sweet potato casserole. The sweet potatoes flesh is pureed with butter and milk, returned to the hollowed-out shells, and topped with mini marshmallows before the final baking.

You can puree the potatoes in a blender or food processor; use the blender for an especially silky texture

4 medium sweet potatoes, washed and halved lengthwise

1/3 cup buttermilk

1/3 cup milk or as needed

4 Tablespoons (½ stick) butter

Freshly ground black pepper

½ cup miniature marshmallows for garnish

Directions

1. Adjust oven rack to lowest position. Preheat oven to 400degrees

2. Place potatoes cut side down on foil or parchment-lined baking sheet. Bake until fork-tender, about 30 minutes. Let cool slightly.

3. Holding a potato half with a pot holder, scoop potato flesh into a blender or food processor, leaving a ¼ - inch shell with remaining potato, set shells aside.

4. With motor running, gradually add both milks to potatoes. Add butter, then process, adding more milk if necessary, until potatoes are silky smooth. Add salt and pepper to taste. Spoon puree back into potato shells. Sprinkle marshmallows over potatoes. Place on baking sheet and bake until potatoes are hot and marshmallows are golden brown, 10 to 12 minutes. Serve hot.

Makes 8 Servings

2 large yams or sweet potatoes

2 Golden Delicious Apples, cored and sliced crosswise into rings

¼ firmly packed brown sugar

1 teaspoon cornstarch

1/8 teaspoon ground cloves

½ cup orange juice

2 Tablespoon chopped pecans or walnuts

Directions

1. Preheat oven to 400 degrees F. Bake yams 50 minutes or until soft but still hold their shape. Let yams cool enough to handle. Reduce oven temperature to 350 degrees F.

2. Peel and slice yams crosswise. In shallow 1-quart baking dish, alternate apple rings and yam slices, over lapping edges slightly. In a small sauce pan combine sugar, cornstarch and cloves; stir in orange juice and mix well. Heat orange juice mixture over medium heat, stirring, until thickened; pour over apples and yams. Sprinkle with nuts; Bake 20 minutes or until apples and yams are tender.

Makes 6 Servings

WILD RICE WITH APRICOTS AND CRANBERRIES

½ cup uncooked wild rice, rinsed and drained

3 cups chicken broth, divided

1 cup apple juice

¾ cup uncooked long-grain rice

½ cup golden raisins

½ cup chopped dried apricots

½ cup dried cranberries

2 Tablespoons butter

¾ cup chopped onion

½ cup coarsely chopped pecans

1/3 cup chopped fresh parsley

Directions

1. Combine wild rice, 1½ cups chicken broth and apple juice in 2-quart saucepan. Bring to a boil over medium-high heat. Reduce heat to low; simmer, covered, about 1 hour or until rice is tender. Drain; set aside.

2. Combine white rice and remaining 1 ½ cups broth in separate 2-quart saucepan. Bring to a boil over medium high heat. Reduce heat to low; simmer, covered, 12 to 15 minutes.

3. Stir in raisins, apricots and cranberries; simmer 5 minutes or until rice is tender and fluffy and liquid is absorbed. Remove from heat. Let stand, covered, 5 minutes or until fruit is tender; set aside.

4. In a large skillet melt butter over medium heat. Add onion; cook and stir 5 to 6 minutes or until tender. Stir in pecans. Cook and stir 2 minutes.

5. Add wild rice and white rice mixtures to skillet. Stir in parsley; cook and stir over medium heat about 2 minutes or until heated through.

Garnish with fresh thyme, orange slices and whole cranberries, if desired.

Makes 6 to 8 Servings

BROCCOLI WITH PARMESAN SAUCE

1½ pounds fresh broccoli

1 cup water

Vegetable cooking spray

¼ cup chopped red pepper

¼ cup chopped onion

1 Tablespoon margarine

2 teaspoons all-purpose flour

¾ cup milk

2 ounces cream cheese

¼ cup grated parmesan cheese

¼ teaspoon garlic powder

Directions

1. Remove tough ends from lower broccoli stalks, and wash thoroughly. Cut into spears. Place broccoli into spears. Place broccoli in a Dutch oven, add water. Bring to a boil, cover, reduce heat, and simmer 10 to 15 minutes or until tender-crisp. Drain; arrange broccoli on a serving platter, keep warm.

2. Coat large nonstick skillet with cooking spray, place over medium heat until hot. Add red pepper and onion; cook, stirring constantly, until tender. Remove from skillet, and set aside.

3. Melt margarine in skillet, stir in flour. Gradually add milk. Cook; stirring constantly: Until slightly thickened. Add reserved onion and red pepper, cream cheese, parmesan cheese and garlic powder; cook over low heat. Stirring constantly: until smooth and thoroughly heated. Spoon over broccoli. Makes 6 servings

1 pound fresh Brussels sprouts

1½ cups water

Vegetable cooking oil

1 teaspoon margarine

1 teaspoon cooking oil

¼ pound fresh mushrooms, sliced

¼ cup coarsely chopped pecans

¼ teaspoon salt

1/8 teaspoon pepper

¼ cup soft whole wheat breadcrumbs

2 Tablespoons grated parmesan cheese

Directions

1. Wash Brussels sprouts thoroughly, remove any discolored leaves. Cut off stem ends, and slash bottom of each sprout with a shallow X.

2. Place Brussels sprouts and water in a medium saucepan; bring to a boil. Cover, reduce heat, and simmer 8 to 10 minutes or until tender-crisp. Drain and set aside.

3. Coat a large nonstick skillet with cooking spray, add margarine and oil. Place over medium high heat until hot. Add mushrooms and pecans, cook, stirring constantly, until mushrooms are tender. Stir in Brussels sprouts. Transfer mixture to an 11 x 7 x 2 inch baking dish.

4. Combine salt, pepper, breadcrumbs and parmesan cheese, stirring well; sprinkle breadcrumb mixture over Brussels sprouts. Broil 4 inches from heat 2 to 3 minutes or until breadcrumbs are golden.

Makes 6 servings

CHEESY MASHED POTATOES WITH GOUDA

1 pound red-skin potatoes cut into 1 ½ inch pieces

1 pound russet potatoes, peeled and cut into 1 ½ inch pieces

¾ cup half-and-half, light cream, or whipping cream

2 cups finely shredded Gouda cheese (8 ounces)

2 green onions or chives

Salt

Freshly ground black pepper

Directions

1. In a 4- to 5-quart Dutch oven or saucepan cook potatoes, covered, in lightly salted boiling water to cover for 20 to 25 minutes or until tender; drain. Return potatoes to Dutch oven.

2. Meanwhile, thinly slice green onions, set aside.

3. Add half-and-half to cooked potatoes. Mash with a potato masher or an electric mixer on low speed until nearly smooth. Stir in 1½ cups of the cheese Season to taste with salt and pepper

4. Transfer mashed potatoes to a serving dish. Sprinkle with green or chives onions and the remaining ½ cup cheese.

Makes 8 Servings

2 ½ pounds russet or Yukon potatoes

1 whole garlic bulb

1 Tablespoon olive oil

½ cup sour cream

2 Tablespoons (¼ stick) butter

1/8 teaspoon salt

1/8 teaspoon pepper

Fresh chives

Directions

1. Preheat oven to 375 degrees F. Peel potatoes and cut into even pieces. Place in a large saucepan of lightly salted water. Bring to a boil. Reduce heat and simmer, about 20 minutes.

2. Meanwhile, separate garlic cloves, but do not peel them. Place in a bowl, add olive oil and toss to coat. Place on a baking sheet and roast until softened, about 10 minutes, allow to cool slightly

3. Drain potatoes and return to saucepan. Mash slightly. Add sour cream and butter. Quickly squeeze pulp from garlic cloves into potatoes. Add salt and pepper.

4. Mash potatoes until combined and smooth. Transfer to a serving bowl. Cut chives into small pieces. Sprinkle over mashed potatoes; serve Makes 4 servings

AU GRATIN POTATOES

4 cups thinly sliced potatoes

1 medium onion, chopped

¼ cup butter

1 tablespoon all-purpose flour

1 teaspoon salt

¼ teaspoon pepper

2 cups milk

2 cups (8-oz.) shredded sharp cheddar cheese, divided

¼ cup fine dry bread crumbs

Paprika

Directions

1. Preheat oven to 325 degrees F.

2. In a 2 quart saucepan, sauté onion in butter until tender. Stir in flour, salt and pepper; cook over low heat until mixture is bubbly, stirring constantly. Remove from heat; gradually stir in milk and 1 ½ cups cheese. Bring to a boil, stirring constantly; cook for 1 minute.

3. In an ungreased 1 ½ quart casserole dish, place potatoes; cover with cheese sauce.

4. Bake, uncovered, for 1 hour.

5. Mix remaining cheese and bread crumbs; sprinkle over potatoes. Sprinkle with paprika.

6. Bake, uncovered, for 15 to 20 minutes, until top is brown and bubbly. Makes 4 servings

PINEAPPLE STUFFED SQUASH

3 medium acorn squash

1 (8-oz) can crushed pineapple, drained

1/3 cup firmly packed brown sugar

3 Tablespoon butter, softened

¼ cup chopped pecans or walnuts

½ teaspoon ground cinnamon

¾ cup water

Lemon twists, optional

Directions

1. Preheat oven to 375 degrees F. Cut squash in half length-wise, and remove seeds; set aside.

2. In a medium bowl, combine pineapple, brown sugar, butter, pecans and cinnamon; mix well. Spoon pineapple mixtures into each squash half. Arrange squash in a 13 x 9 x 2-inch baking dish add ¾ cup water. Cover and bake at 375 degrees F. for 50 minutes. . Uncover and bake an additional 10 minutes. Garnish with lemon twits, if desired.

Makes 6 servings

GREEN BEANS AND BRAISED CELERY

2 pounds fresh green beans

1 bunch celery hearts

¼ cup butter

4 or 5 Tablespoons chicken broth

Salt and pepper to taste

1 teaspoon lemon juice

1 (4-oz) jar whole pimientos, drained and diced

Directions

1. Wash beans, trim ends and remove strings. In a Dutch oven or large saucepan, bring 4 cups water to a boil. Add beans; cook uncovered, for 10 minutes or until crisp-tender. Drain, and plunge beans into cold water. Drain and set aside.

2. Cut celery into 4 to 5-inch long pieces. Melt ¼ cup butter in a large skillet; add broth; and bring to a boil. Add celery, salt and pepper; cover and cook for 5 minutes or until tender. Drain.

3. Melt 3 Tablespoons butter, add green beans, lemon juice (season with more salt and pepper if desired) Heat beans thoroughly, stirring gently.

4. Arrange green beans and celery on a serving platter. Garnish with pimientos.

Makes 8 servings

If you prefer use butter or coconut oil instead of the reduced-calorie margarine

2 (10-oz) pkg. frozen chopped spinach, thawed

6 ounces light cream cheese, softened

1 Tablespoon reduced-calorie margarine, softened

¼ cup skim milk

1 (9-oz) pkg. frozen artichoke hearts, thawed and chopped

3 Tablespoons oil-free Italian dressing

1 (12-oz) jar diced pimiento, drained

¼ teaspoon black pepper

Vegetable cooking spray

2 Tablespoons grated fat-free Parmesan Italian topping

Directions

1. Drain spinach, and press between paper towels to remove access moisture; set aside.

2. Combine cream cheese and margarine in a bowl; beat at medium speed with an electric mixer until creamy. Gradually add milk, beating well. Stir in spinach, artichoke hearts, Italian dressing, pimientos and pepper.

3. Spoon into a 1-quart casserole coated with cooking spray; sprinkle with Italian topping. Cover; bake at 350 degrees F. for 30 minutes. Uncover; bake 10 additional minutes.

Makes Six – ½ cup servings

BROCCOLI-CAULIFLOWER TOSS

4 cups cauliflower florets

2 cups small broccoli florets

1 (2-oz) jar diced pimiento, drained

¾ cup plain non-fat yogurt

3 Tablespoons minced fresh parsley

2 Tablespoons grated Parmesan cheese

1 Tablespoon Dijon-style mustard

¼ teaspoon garlic powder

1/8 teaspoon white pepper

Directions

1. Arrange cauliflower and broccoli in a vegetable steamer over boiling water. Cover and steam 4 minutes or until crisp-tender. Drain well. Transfer to a serving bowl; add pimiento and toss well. Set aside and keep warm.

2. Combine yogurt and remaining ingredients. Pour yogurt mixture over vegetables; toss gently.

Makes 6 one cup servings

LEMON BAKED ASPARAGUS

Vegetable cooking spray

2 pounds asparagus, trimmed

1 Tablespoon olive oil

Freshly ground black pepper

½ cup Vegetable Broth

3 ounces soft goat cheese, crumbled

1 Tablespoon lemon juice

1 teaspoon grated lemon peel

Directions

1. Heat the oven to 425°F. Spray a 17 x 11-inch roasting pan or shallow baking sheet with the cooking spray.

2. Stir the asparagus and olive oil in the pan; season with the black pepper. Pour in the broth.

3. Roast the asparagus for 20 minutes or until it's tender, stirring once during cooking. Top with the cheese, lemon juice and lemon peel.

Makes 4 servings

QUINOA SALAD

1 cup quinoa

1½ cups water

2 packed cups kale, chopped into bite-sized pieces

Juice from 1 lemon

¼ cup olive oil

½ teaspoon salt

1 cup pomegranate seeds

1 Haas avocado, chopped

½ cup onion, minced

¼ cup additional olive oil

Directions

1. Rinse quinoa and drain with a fine mesh strainer or cheese cloth.

Cook the quinoa 1½ cups water. To cook quinoa on the stove, put the quinoa and water in a 2 quart pot and bring to a boil. Lower the heat and simmer for 15 minutes. When the quinoa is cooked, transfer to the large serving bowl.

2. Meanwhile in a separate bowl, combine the kale, lemon juice, olive oil, and salt. Get in there with your hands and massage the kale so it's well coated, and set it aside to wilt for at least 10 minutes.

3. When the quinoa has cooled, transfer the kale mixture, pomegranate seeds, avocado, onion, and additional olive oil to the bowl with the quinoa, and toss well. You can serve immediately or make this salad a day ahead and refrigerate overnight.

Makes 4 servings

SUNFLOWER CHICKEN SALAD

Sunflower seeds and cheese distinguish this chicken salad from the rest. Tossed with grapes and celery in a basic mayonnaise dressing

2 cups cubed cooked chicken breast meat

1 cup cubed Cheddar cheese

¼ cup sunflower seeds

¼ cup thinly sliced celery

½ cup seedless green grapes, halved

½ cup mayonnaise

Salt and pepper to taste

Directions

In a large bowl combine the chicken, cheese, sunflower seeds, celery, grapes, mayonnaise and salt and pepper to taste. Mix all together and serve on rolls or lettuce leaves, if desired.

8 large sweet potatoes (5 ½ pounds)

4 granny smith apples

4 green onions

Poppy seed dressing

Directions

1. Cook potatoes in boiling water to cover for 25 to 30 minutes or until tender; drain and cool. Peel sweet potatoes, and cut into ½-inch thick slices. Cut apples into thin wedges; slice green onions.

2. Arrange one-fourth sweet potato slices, apple wedges, and green onions in a large bowl; drizzle with one-fourth poppy seed dressing.

3. Repeat layers 3 times with remaining ingredients; cover and chill.

Makes 12 to 15 servings

CONTENTS

BROCCOLI-CAULIFLOWER TOSS   90

LEMON BAKED ASPARAGUS   91

SALADS92

UINOA SALAD   92

SUNFLOWER CHICKEN SALAD   94

SWEET POTATO-APPLE SALAD 95

Made in the USA
Lexington, KY
09 December 2016